Constipation Relief & Gut Healing Cookbook

SWH Medial LLC.

www.NaturalConstipationSolutions.com

© 2019 Wendy Hayden

All rights reserved.

No portion of this book may be reproduced in any form without permission from the publisher, except as permitted by U.S. copyright law.

Constipation is becoming an epidemic, even in children. Over 15% of the population is struggling with constipation, leading to over 6 million doctor's visits and 700,000 emergency room visits a year. Often when you go to the doctor for constipation, you are given a laxative and sent home. Laxatives are just a bandaid on the symptom of constipation and don't address the root cause of constipation.

Diet is a very common culprit of chronic constipation. Diets of highly processed, GMO food that is sprayed with glyphosate and other herbicides can wreak havoc on our gut health leading to constipation and leaky gut. Antibiotics prescribed by our doctors, and in our food, are killing off our gut bacteria making it hard for us to digest our food. Many common laxatives, like PEG 3350, the only ingredient in Miralax, can also kill off our gut bacteria. No wonder so many people are struggling with constipation!

It can be hard to change your diet and even harder to change your child's diet. But there are kid and picky-eater friendly food options that can bring immediate relief from constipation and can help heal your gut, all while tasting great.

Often when people have a self restricted diet, the foods that they do eat are the ones that are causing their constipation. Some foods, especially gluten and dairy, can have an addictive quality in some people that makes them crave them.

When I suggest cutting gluten or dairy from someone's diet, I am often met with shock and told that they love that food too much to even imagine cutting it out. Or they may tell me that their child only eats foods that contain gluten or dairy so their child wouldn't have anything left to eat if they eliminated gluten and dairy.

Gluten and dairy can work almost like opiates, in some people. They have proteins in them that fit in the opiate receptors. When you eliminate those foods, often kids will branch out and try new foods.

Children with sensory issues often struggle with food textures. Preparing food in different ways can get someone who "doesn't like" a certain food to love it. They might not be willing to try a cooked vegetable but might enjoy it raw or chop into small pieces or mashed.

Try serving foods cooked, raw, hot, cold, mashed, canned, fresh or frozen and see which one your child is most receptive to. There was a period of time when my sensory kid wouldn't eat fresh blueberries but loved frozen ones.

Even picky adults can be more open to foods when presented differently.

Some of the recipes in this book are super tasty like my famous Coconut Oil Poop candies. But some are different, like my fermented carrots. You might think that you or your child won't like them but you might be surprised!

My supertaster son absolutely adores fermented carrots and will ask me to make them for him. And my very picky eater husband loves my fermented salsa.

Included in this book are recipes that will help produce a bowel movement quickly, recipes that will repopulate your gut flora and ones that help heal your gut.

As important as it is to add healthy foods to your diet, it can be just as important, or even more important, to remove foods that are causing constipation issues.

Gluten, dairy, soy, corn, processed foods, white foods like white rice, white bread, or red meat can cause constipation in certain people. Doing an elimination diet can really help you to figure out what is causing your constipation.

To do an elimination diet take out your suspected problem foods for a month or two and see if your constipation improves, then add each food back in and see if your constipation worsens. Dairy can take two months to get completely out of your system.

Tracking your bowel movements can help you to figure out what is causing problems and what is helping. I have a free bowel movement tracker that you can download at:

https://naturalconstipationsolutions.com/bowel-movement-tracker/

I have a lot of resources to help you figure out what is causing your constipation on my website. NaturalConstipationSolutions.com

If your child is struggling with constipation and a change of diet isn't enough to help them overcome it, my books "What Your Doctor Didn't Tell You About Childhood Constipation" or "Overcome Your Child's Constipation" can help you to get to the root cause of their constipation.

I have also written two children's books that might help your young child. "Dash's Belly Ache" is a book for children who are struggling with constipation or withholding. My book "Dash is a New Fooder!" is for picky eaters, kids with limited diets or for children who need to make changes to their diets.

I hope you find some recipes in this book that help you get relief from chronic constipation for you or your child.

Wendy Hayden

Drinks

Electrolyte Drink for Constipation Relief

This homemade Electrolyte Drink for Constipation Relief has a very strong laxative effect. This drink has a salty taste that might take some getting used to but it is very effective for constipation relief.

It may surprise you that not only might your child drink it, but they may even start craving it because of the salt and minerals in it. This drink is a wonderful alternative to toxic laxatives like Miralax. My son had terrible side effects from Miralax which led me to learn of safe alternatives.

I make this for my husband who has Crohn's. Because his gut is so damaged by the disease and from all of the surgeries he's had, his electrolytes are often really off.

We found that he was not healing after a surgery he had due to being salt deficient. Once we added this drink into his daily regimen, he began healing. This drink also ended his debilitating muscle cramps which would wake him up screaming in the middle of the night.

We do not use Gatorade or other drinks like that because they have many ingredients in them like food colors and preservatives.

Many of my readers have used this drink with their children with great success and have gotten their children to have a daily bowel movement when they drink this drink.

My reader, Courtney Tapper said, "We are recovering from the stomach flu and the homemade electrolyte drink is AMAZING as my girls won't eat or drink and I was worried…..but this got their tummies moving and was gentle on their sore throats."

I use a large glass or a ball jar and put in one cup of Orange Juice but you could experiment with other juices your family likes.

This electrolyte drink very strong laxative effect usually starts to work in minutes but if you are very deficient in these minerals it might take longer and more of the drink to have the desired effect.

You can drink multiple recipes worth if you are attempting to do a cleanout.

You might need to start with a lower amount of the ingredients and work up to the level that works for you or your child or try different ratios depending on what you are most deficient in.

Celtic Sea Salt for Constipation Relief

I recommend using Celtic Sea Salt. Do not use table salt which may be bleached and have aluminum in it.

Celtic Sea Salt has over 80 trace minerals in addition to sodium. It is non-GMO, Kosher, Gluten-Free and doesn't have any caking agents. We used Himalayan salt for years but found the Celtic Sea Salt to work much better for our health and it tastes amazing.

Celtic Sea Salt is what we use for our main salt. We salt everything with it. I love the crunchy texture and I think it is more flavorful than other salt products.

You could use Himalayan Salt but I have found that the Celtic works much better for constipation relief and for gut healing.

Epsom Salt

You can leave out the Epsom salt if you or your child doesn't like the taste but Epsom salt has a laxative effect. It is a great source of magnesium and sulfur. Almost everyone is chronically deficient in both magnesium and sulfur.

If you don't want to use Epsom salt for some reason you can use a few drops of Omniblue Ocean Minerals or mix some Natural Calm Magnesium Citrate up with hot water and then add it to the drink instead.

You can put this drink over ice, or blend it with ice to make a fun drink. You can make a slushie with this drink to make a really fun way to get your child to drink this drink.

You will need to experiment with how much is needed for you or for your child to have 1-3 bowel movements each day.

If you are using this for your child, I recommend drinking it along with him or her so you will understand how it affects them as it can be very powerful.

We have been taught to be scared of salt but the first thing that happens when you go to the hospital is that they put you on a saline (saltwater) drip.

We need salt. Salt is necessary for many of the chemical reactions that support enzyme function, hormone production, and protein transport. But we need high-quality salt with trace minerals. Not table salt that has aluminum and is bleached.

New research is showing that low sodium diets are not good for people. Not even people with high blood pressure.

Natural Electrolyte Drink for Constipation Relief Recipe

1/2 to 1 tsp of Celtic Sea Salt

1/4 Tsp Organic Epsom Salt (make sure it says safe for internal use or has directions for laxative use on the package)

1/8 tsp Non-GMO Cream of Tartar (potassium)

Add 1 1/2 cups of cold water.

Mix together and refrigerate or pour over ice.

Everyone is different in how much they will need to drink for this to be effective in producing a bowel movement. It could take 4 ounces or 4 recipes worth. If you are very constipated or are very deficient in the minerals in the drink, then it will take more to reach bowel tolerance. As time goes on, you may find that you need to drink less to have the same effect.

Apple Cider Vinegar Drink for Reflux and GERD

My son struggled with reflux from infancy. His pediatrician diagnosed him with Reflux at just a few weeks old. My son was very fussy and seemed to be in a lot of pain in the first few months of his life from his reflux but I could keep it mostly under control with gripe water.

When my son was 16 months old he was hospitalized with Salmonella and was put on IV antibiotics. When he got out of the hospital, his reflux was awful.

His pediatrician told me to give him Pepcid. I regret following her advice and giving him Pepcid. Pepcid is an acid reducer. This sounds good in theory but in practice, we need stomach acid to digest our food, kill harmful bacteria and parasites, and absorb nutrients from our food.

When your stomach doesn't have enough acid, the lower esophageal sphincter that closes your stomach off from your esophagus isn't triggered to close properly, resulting in reflux symptoms as the acid travels up your esophagus, instead of staying in your stomach.

My son had constipation from birth, but the combination of antibiotics and using an acid reducer caused his constipation to worsen exponentially. This led to his gastroenterologist prescribing Miralax which caused a whole host of side effects that took us years to undo.

When I took him off of Miralax and Pepcid, I did a lot of research into safe, natural alternatives to help him with his reflux and constipation. Apple Cider Vinegar kept coming up over and over again as the more effective natural remedy for reflux.

Apple Cider Vinegar is a vinegar that is naturally fermented and contains "The Mother." The mother is the bacteria and yeast that ferment the apples. The bacteria is very beneficial to gut health

ACV helps with Reflux and GERD by increasing the amount of stomach acid you have, and even though it is an acid, it alkalizes your system which is very beneficial to your digestion.

I wanted to try ACV with my son but couldn't imagine getting him to drink it as it is very sour.

My son was a very picky eater and a super-taster with sensory issues. ACV has a very strong sour taste and even a lot of adults do not like the taste of it.

I developed this recipe to get my son to willingly drink his daily dose of ACV. Not only did it end his reflux but the beneficial bacteria in the ACV helped to heal his gut, repopulate the bacteria killed off by antibiotics and Miralax, and helped him to digest his food better.

My dad was also dealing with reflux and had been put on acid reducers by his doctor. I convinced him to try ACV and it floored him at how much better he felt. My dad quickly got off of the acid reducers and has been using ACV for years to combat reflux symptoms.

I hope this recipe for this really tasty, kid-friendly drink helps you or your child to overcome reflux and GERD.

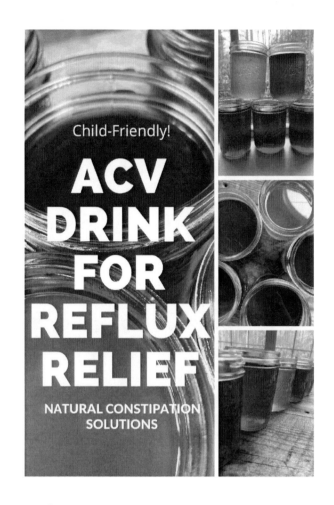

ACV Drink for Reflux Relief

Celestial Seasonings Herbal Tea Sampler or other herbal teas

Bragg's Apple Cider Vinegar, or other ACV with The Mother.

Organic Honey or Organic Sugar

The Celestial Seasonings Herbal Tea Sampler has 5 different flavors of herbal tea. This is a great choice because you can try all the flavors and see which one you or your child likes best.

It has Wild Berry Zinger, Raspberry Zinger, Country Peach Passion, Black Cherry Berry, and True Blueberry teas. My son loves the Raspberry and Wild Berry Zingers. The teas are very colorful, which is super appealing to picky kids. This drink is very kid-friendly and almost tastes like Kool-aid or fruit punch but without the chemicals.

Of course, you can use any herbal teas that you or your child would enjoy. My recommendation is just one of many options.

For each drink:

Boil 1 cup water.

Add 1 teabag to a cup or heat-proof glass and add 1 cup of boiling water. Steep

Add 1-2 teaspoons of ACV depending on taste.

Add 1-2 teaspoons of sugar or honey, depending on taste.

Add ice and drink.

I would use a straw when drinking this Reflux Relief Drink as ACV can cause damage to the enamel on your teeth if you drink it frequently without using a straw.

Chia Fresca

Chia Fresca is a great drink to combat dehydration, which is a very common cause of constipation and fun, refreshing way to add fiber to your diet.

The Aztecs of Mexico used chia seeds as a superfood to keep up their energy on long journeys or when running many miles. Chia seeds are high in Omega 3 fatty acids, magnesium, protein, and fiber.

This fun limeade drink is common in many parts of Mexico.

Once the chia seeds are hydrated they develop a gel-like coating on the outside. This gel helps the chia seeds move through your digestive system, moving the stool and helping you to eliminate it.

The drink has a fun texture almost like Boba tea.

Ingredients:

Juice of 1 lime

2 cups cold water

1 tsp honey

1 pinch of Himalayan or Celtic sea salt

1 TBS Chia Seeds

Add all ingredients to a glass and stir, making sure the chia seeds do not clump.

Let sit 10-15 minutes to let chia seeds absorb the water.

Drink immediately or refrigerate and stir before drinking.

Garnish with sliced limes, lemons or sliced cucumbers.

Almond Milk

Dairy is a common cause of constipation. You can buy non-dairy milk at the grocery store but it is very easy to make at home. When you make it yourself you have complete control over the ingredients.

A Double-Blind Cross Over Trial was done with 65 children struggling with chronic constipation to see if Cow's Milk Protein was causing their constipation.

https://www.ncbi.nlm.nih.gov/pmc/articles/PMC3571647/

Half of the children were given cow's milk for the first two weeks and the other half were given soy milk for the first two weeks, without being told which one they were getting.

They all then had two weeks of being soy milk and cow's milk-free, followed by two weeks where the children who were originally given cow's milk were switched to soy and the children who were given soy were switched to cow's milk.

Constipation resolved for 68% of the children drinking soy milk, but none of the children drinking cow's milk.

Beyond constipation, other signs of dairy intolerance are bloating, abdominal cramping, gas, fat in the stool, acne, seasonal allergies or congestion, and skin rashes or eczema. If you are struggling with constipation and other symptoms of dairy intolerance,

I recommend strictly eliminating all dairy for at least 60 days. It takes at least 60 days to get all of the cow's milk protein out of your system. When you add dairy back in, it will usually be very obvious if dairy is a cause of your constipation.

Almond Milk Recipe

Soak 1 cup of Organic Raw Almonds overnight or for up to two days in non-chlorinated water.

Drain the water off the soaked almonds and rinse in clean water.

Put your soaked almonds in a high powered blender. I use my Vitamix, but any high powered blender will work. If you make it in a regular blender it will still work but will have a grittier texture.
Add two cups of water and blend on the highest speed for 2 minutes. Strain the mixture either with a fine mesh strainer or a nut milk bag.

You can drink it as is or add a small amount of sweetener or a bit of Vanilla extract.

Refrigerate.

Homemade nut milk does not last as long in the fridge as store-bought because it is not pasteurized and does not have preservatives. It will last 2 or 3 days instead of a week but you are not consuming preservatives.

It is simple and quick to make so you can make small batches as needed.

Natural Constipation Solutions

Homemade Almond Milk

Recipe at NaturalConstipationSolutions.com

Fermented Limeade or Lemonade

This recipe can be customized for you or your child's taste. You can use lemon, lime, oranges, cucumber, ginger, and mint or just one, two or three of these ingredients depending on what you or your child likes.

My son loves limes so we usually use that as a base. He also loves mint but isn't as fond of ginger. Ginger is great for gastro issues though so if your child likes ginger ale, it is worth trying this recipe with the ginger.

Fermented Limeade or Lemonade Made with Probiotics

2 liters of water

1 medium cucumber, peeled and thinly sliced

1 lemon or lime, juiced

1 lemon or lime sliced

1-4 capsules of probiotics

1 teaspoon freshly grated ginger

10-12 mint leaves

1 TBS organic sugar or honey

Add 2 liters of water to a container. Add your choice of peeled cucumber slices, lime or lemon juice, sliced lemon, freshly grated ginger, mint leaves, and sugar or honey.

Steep overnight on the counter and then put it in the fridge until it is cold or serve over ice. You can also make a slushie by straining out the solids and blend with ice.

Fermented Soda

To make fermented ginger ale you must have what is called a Ginger Bug. This is the starter for the soda.

Ginger Bug Recipe

Ingredients:

    1 large piece of fresh organic ginger, approximately 3-5 inches.

    5 tbsp sugar

    3 1/4 cups of water (chlorine-free)

Finely dice 1 tbsp of ginger. Don't peel the ginger because the skin helps with fermentation.

Mix all of the water with 1 tbsp of sugar and 1 tbsp of grated ginger in a glass quart jar. Stir until the sugar is dissolved.

Cover with a cloth (or coffee filter) and secure in place with a rubber band or string.

Place the jar somewhere warm and dark to ferment, such as a kitchen cupboard.

Every day add 1 tablespoon of diced ginger and 1 tablespoon of sugar.

After 2-3 days it should start to bubble. Once it is really bubbly (about 5 days) you are ready to make ginger ale or other naturally fermented sodas.

To keep the bug alive and continue growing it, you will need to feed it regularly.

To feed your Ginger Bug:

Add 1 teaspoon minced ginger and 1 teaspoon sugar per day if kept at room temperature.

You can also "rest" it in the fridge and feed it 1 Tablespoon each of ginger and sugar once a week. To reactivate it, remove and let it reach room temperature and begin feeding it again.

Ginger Ale Recipe

5 cups filtered water +4 cups filtered water

1 1/4 cup sugar

4-6 inches ginger root

2 tbsp fresh or bottled lemon juice

Syrup

When your ginger bug is ready and bubbly, you are ready to make the syrup for your soda.

In a medium saucepan add 5 cups water, 1 ¼ cup sugar, and 4'-6' of ginger root, chopped or grated.

Bring to a boil until the sugar is dissolved. Simmer for about 15 minutes.

Let cool completely before proceeding to the next step so it doesn't kill your ginger bug.

Add 2 TBS lemon juice.

Strain your syrup and ginger bug to get out ginger pieces.

Pour strained syrup and ginger bug into a large glass jar along with 4 cups filtered water (or two jars if you need to, depending on the size jar you have.) Cap jar.

Set out of the direct sun on the counter or in the cupboard and stir once a day.

When you start to see bubbles when you stir, it is ready to bottle.

Pour your mix into glass bottles with lids that can be sealed or tightened. Ball jars or bottles with hasp lids that can be sealed.

Leave about 1-inch space at the top.

Seal the bottle tightly.

Burp bottle one time a day to release pressure.

Let bottles sit on your counter approximately two more days depending on the temperature of your kitchen. When you're burping the bottles and hear a pop or see that it's fizzy, you know its ready.

Transfer to the fridge. Once cold, enjoy it!

Switchel

Switchel is a drink made with ginger. It uses apple cider vinegar for the ferment. You are getting the benefit of the ginger, which helps with digestion, gas and bloating, along with the benefits of ACV, beneficial bacteria. This drink is great for alkalizing your system and helping with digestion.

Switchel is also much easier to make than fermented ginger ale.

Ingredients:

- 2 quarts filtered water
- 1/2 cup raw apple cider vinegar with the mother
- ¼-½ cup honey, sweeten to taste. Local honey is the best choice
- 2 tsp ground ginger

Place all ingredients together in a large pitcher and mix. You can add ice and drink the switchel immediately at this point if you like.

Or

Leave the sealed bottles on the counter for at least 2-3 days to add carbonation and then refrigerate.

Constipation Relief Coffee

Coffee has a laxative effect on many people. The caffeine in coffee stimulates the intestines and can cause a bowel movement but even decaffeinated coffee can cause a bowel movement.

Warm or hot beverages like coffee or tea open up the blood vessels in the intestines and cause more blood to flow which causes increased motility in the GI tract.

Coffee also acidifies the stomach which helps with digestion. Coffee triggers the distal colon to expel stool.

When you add in coconut oil or MCT oil, you have a drink with a very strong laxative effect.

Brew one cup of coffee

Add 1TBS organic Coconut Oil or MCT oil

Blend in a blender or use a stick blender to froth the oil in the coffee. This will form a frothy head on your coffee. If you do not blend the oil into the coffee, the oil will sit on the surface of the coffee and not be as palatable even though it will still work for constipation relief.

Fiber

Chia Pudding

Chia Pudding is a great option for fiber and constipation relief and is kid-friendly.

It can be tricky, especially with a less than ideal diet, to get enough dietary fiber to prevent constipation. A half-cup of cooked veggies has 2-4 grams and a small piece of fruit has about 3 grams of fiber.

Children need 19-25 grams of fiber a day, women need 25 grams of fiber a day and men need 38, so you can see that it can be difficult to get enough from a standard diet. It is almost impossible to get enough with a processed food diet made up of white flour and rice.

If you are gluten-free, most gluten-free baked goods are lower in fiber than the wheat flour versions because gluten-free flours are often filled with starches that are low in fiber.

Fiber supplements are one option to get more fiber but I usually prefer to use food over supplements if at all possible.

Chia Seeds are a wonderful source of fiber and magnesium, both helpful for constipation.

One of my favorite ways to get easily digestible fiber in my child's diet is with chia seeds.

Chia seeds have 11 grams of fiber in just two Tablespoons!

2 TBS also contains 30% of your RDA of magnesium and a great ratio of Omega 3 to Omega 6 fatty acids. They have been used since Mayan times when Mayan warriors ate them for strength and endurance.

Chia seeds are very high in magnesium, 80mg in 2 TBS. Magnesium is a critical mineral for constipation and most of us are deficient in it.

How to introduce Chia for constipation relief

When introducing chia seeds to the diet, start slowly until you know how you or your child will handle them.

Fiber can sometimes cause increased constipation in some people so monitor closely to see if adding fiber is helping or making the situation worse.

One of my favorite ways to incorporate chia is with chia seed pudding. This pudding is a very versatile base that you can customize depending on your taste preference. It is also really fun and tasty which is great if you are trying to get fiber into your constipated child.

I start with a very simple chia pudding made with canned full-fat coconut milk. You get the benefit of the coconut milk as well as the chia seeds.

If you or your child won't or can't eat coconut milk, then use any nut or seed milk will work if you are dairy-free or cow's milk if you are able to tolerate dairy. (most people with constipation issues do so much better when they are dairy-free.)

Coconut Milk Chia Pudding Recipe for Fiber and Constipation Relief

1 can of Organic Full Fat Coconut Milk in a BPA free can (Amazon Links)

1/3 cup of Organic Chia Seeds

1-2 tsp of Organic Vanilla depending on taste

1-2 TBS of Grade A Organic Maple Syrup or Organic Raw Honey, depending on taste

Mix in a bowl and then transfer to storage containers. I use small ball jars for individual servings. Keep in the fridge for at least 30 minutes or overnight before serving and up to 3 days after you make them.

Other Options for Chia Pudding

If you or your child doesn't like the texture of the chia pudding you can try grinding up the chia seeds before making the pudding.

Once you have your base of pudding you can customize it. Add your favorite fruits, nuts or seeds, drizzle with honey or more maple syrup. You can add cocoa powder, pureed fruit, or peanut butter before you mix them up. Add mini chocolate chips or shredded coconut.

Divide your batch and mix cocoa powder in half and peanut butter in half and then make layered parfaits by adding one layer to the jar, refrigerate until firm and then add the second layer.

Flaxseed Prune Applesauce

Flaxseed is very high in fiber, especially soluble fiber, which is very helpful for constipation. Flaxseed is also high in Omega 3 fatty acids.

You can buy flaxseed ground or whole. If possible, buy whole flaxseed and grind it before use as the flaxseeds as they lose their nutritional value quickly. I use a coffee grinder that I only use for herbs and seeds to grind flax seeds. Store your flaxseed in the refrigerator.

You can sprinkle flax seeds in yogurt, add them to any baked goods you make, or add to smoothies as well as use them in this recipe.

Prune juice has been used for generations for constipation. Prunes are high in soluble and insoluble fiber and they contain sorbitol which draws fluids into the intestines softening the stool, making it easier to pass. The skins of prunes contain dihydroxyphenylisatin which stimulates intestinal movement.

Apples are also high in fiber and contain sorbitol which acts as an osmotic.

Putting apples, prunes, and flaxseed together can be very helpful if your constipation is caused by a lack of fiber or if you struggle with hard to pass stools.

Make sure you drink a lot of fluids when eating this or any high fiber foods as the fiber can dry out the stool and worsen constipation in some people.

If you notice a worsening of constipation, cut back on fiber until you get your constipation under control by other methods and then add fiber back into your diet as you can tolerate it.

Ingredients:

- 1 cup Prune juice
- 4 apples
- 2 TBS ground flaxseeds

Instructions:

Chop your apples into small chunks.

Put chopped apples into a medium saucepan and add 1 cup prune juice. Cook over low heat until the apples break down into apple sauce, stirring regularly.

Remove from heat and add 2 TBS ground flaxseeds. Stir to make sure the flaxseeds don't clump. Let sit until the flaxseed absorbs the liquid in the apple sauce. If the apple sauce gets too thick, add more prune juice. Serve warm or cold.

High Fiber Beet Smoothie

Smoothies and smoothie bowls are a great way to get a lot of healthy, high fiber fruits and vegetables into your diet and are kid-friendly. I like this beet smoothie because you can get a lot of fiber and nutrition in one serving.

Beets are high in fiber, magnesium, potassium, and antioxidants. Beets also increase enzyme activity in the liver, thinning bile and aiding digestion. They also add beautiful red color to the smoothie.

Ginger is wonderful for constipation and helps reduce gas in the digestive system. Ginger is anti-inflammatory and supports bile production.

Soaked chia seeds are high in fiber and help move the stool along in your digestive tract.

High-quality yogurt or kefir, either dairy-based or dairy-free depending on your tolerance for dairy products add beneficial bacteria to your gut. Fermented foods help repopulate gut bacteria which helps combat constipation.

Spinach is very high in iron and fiber. Smoothies are a great place to hide greens like spinach if you are trying to get more greens into your child or a greens resistant adult.

Ingredients:

1 large cooked beet. Chop unpeeled beet and put in a pot of water. Cook over medium heat for 15-20 minutes until center of beets are soft.

1 inch of peeled ginger

1 cup yogurt or kefir

1 TBS soaked chia seeds. Take 1 TBS of chia seeds and add 3 TBS of water. Let sit 15 minutes until a gel forms.

½ cup spinach

1 TBS honey

Add all of the ingredients to your blender and blend until smooth.

Green Smoothie

Ingredients:

1 cup fresh spinach

2 tablespoons chopped fresh cilantro

1-inch of ginger root

1/2 cup water

1 cup diced cucumber

1 medium green apple diced

1 tablespoon of lemon juice

1–3 tsp MCT Oil

Instructions:

Place spinach, cilantro, ginger, and water into a blender jar. Blend until smooth and leafy chunks are gone.

Add cucumber, apple, lemon juice, and MCT oil to blender.

Blend again until smooth.

Constipation Relieving Smoothie Bowl

Ingredients:

1 ½ cups canned full-fat coconut milk

1 cup of frozen berries

¼ cup MCT oil

2 tablespoons Chia Seeds

1 tablespoon apple cider vinegar

1 teaspoon vanilla extract

Optional:

Shredded coconut

Almonds

Hemp hearts

Fresh berries

Instructions:

Place coconut milk, frozen berries, MCT oil, Chia seeds, ACV and vanilla in the blender or bowl of your food processor. Blend until smooth.

Divide between 3 bowls.

Optional: Top with shredded coconut, hemp hearts, or fresh berries.

Ferments

Cultured Butter

Many people with chronic constipation can't tolerate dairy. But some can still tolerate butter even if they can't tolerate other forms of dairy such as milk or ice cream.

If you or your child can tolerate butter, it is so much better for you than margarine or other butter substitutes. If you buy butter look for an organic or grass-fed brand such as Kerry Gold or Amish butter made by local dairies.

Making butter is a fun project to do with your kids. When you make cultured butter, you are making a kid-friendly way to get lots of good bacteria into your family.

Ingredients

1-pint organic whipping cream

1-2 capsules of high-quality probiotics

Celtic Sea Salt

I try to only use organic grass-fed whipping cream. I have used Horizon Organic Whipping Cream, and it worked, but I prefer to use one from a local dairy or health food store that isn't ultra-pasteurized.

Pour the cream into a glass jar.

I add one to two capsules of probiotic powder. Open the capsules and pour the powdered probiotic into the cream.

Stir.

Cover the jar with a towel or a coffee filter.

This is the part that will make most people cringe…leave the cream out on your counter overnight.

What!? It'll go bad!

Actually, it won't. It will grow good bacteria that are beneficial to your gut.

Leave it out at room temperature for 12-24 hours. I usually do this after dinner and make the butter when I wake up in the morning. The longer you leave it within that time frame, the more bacteria will grow, and the tangier the butter will be.

I find that about 12-15 hours is just about right. It could take longer or less time depending on how warm or cool you keep your house.

After your cream is fermented, pour the cream into your mixer or food processor.

Turn the mixer up as high as it can go before it starts splattering the cream. It will begin to whip the cream and then you will notice that it will start to separate.

The butter curds will separate from the buttermilk.

It's really exciting and kids will think it is super fun.

Pour the butter and buttermilk through a wire mesh strainer over a mixing bowl.

Press all of the buttermilk out of the butter. I use a rubber spatula to press the butter against the mesh.

After removing as much buttermilk as possible manually, run the strainer under the faucet to wash the buttermilk out. Keep pressing until no creamy liquid comes out. If you leave buttermilk in the butter it will go bad quickly.

You can use the buttermilk in biscuits, pancakes or salad dressing. You can add Celtic Sea Salt to taste at this point or garlic or herbs if you want.Put the butter into a glass jar and store in the refrigerator.

Lacto-Fermented Salsa

There are no exact measurements in this recipe. I know that will be frustrating for some. But so much depends on how spicy you like your salsa and how hot your particular batch of peppers are.

We grow our own jalapeño and poblano peppers and it is always amazing to me how different the heat levels can be when the peppers are from the same seeds and grown in the same way. How hot or dry the growing season has been, does seem to impact the level of heat in the peppers.

But the good news is that you really can't screw it up! No matter what you do, it is going to taste amazing. Just taste test the salsa as you add the hot peppers to see when you have reached the heat level you like.

Ingredients

>   2-3LBS of Organic Tomatoes
>
>   1-5 hot peppers. I used 4 jalapeños and one poblano
>
>   2 heads of garlic chopped or 2 TBS of chopped jarred garlic.
>
>   1 bunch fresh cilantro chopped, approximately 1 cup
>
>   2 TBS Celtic Sea Salt

Start with 2-3 pounds of tomatoes. I used a mixture of tomatoes on the vine and plum tomatoes. In the summer, I get my tomatoes from our garden which is the best.

I wasn't making this salsa in the winter because I didn't think it would taste as good with store-bought tomatoes. I was looking for a good way to up the good bacteria in my husband's gut, and I knew he loved this salsa, so I thought I would try it with store-bought produce. He and I were both surprised at how good it tasted. So don't let the season stop you from trying this recipe.

Chop the tomatoes, peppers, cilantro and 2 heads of garlic or 2 TBS of bottled organic garlic.

Put in a large mixing bowl. Add 1 1/2-2 TBS of Celtic Sea Salt.

Stir together.

I avoid using metal when making ferments so I use a large pyrex mixing bowl and a wooden spoon.

Put the salsa into clean pint glass jars. I boil water in a large pot and put the jars in the boiling water for 5 minutes to sanitize them

Once you put the salsa in the jars, take your wooden spoon and push all of the veggies down into the liquid brine.

Put a coffee filter or clean towel over each jar and tie with string, use a rubber band or just let sit loosely.

The jars can sit on your counter for 24 hours up to 3 days.

Taste-test daily to see when it tastes good to you. You will see bubbles form in the salsa. That is the bacteria doing its job. The longer you ferment the more bacteria but the salsa can start to taste sour if you leave it fermenting for too long.

If you see white mold, then you need to start over but bubbles are what you want.

The warmer the weather or the hotter your kitchen the quicker they will ferment.

Once you reach the amount of fermenting you like, put lids on your jars and store in your fridge for up to a week.

Lacto-Fermented Pickled Cucumbers and Carrots

4 cups of filtered water

2 tablespoons Celtic Sea Salt

1 pound carrots, cut into sticks or cucumbers cut into spears or slices.

Cabbage leaves (for the top of the ferment) or canning weights

1 TBS chopped garlic

1 TBS chopped dill

Instructions:

Clean and dry your jars and lids. I boil water in a large pot and put the jars in boiling water for 5 minutes.

In a large mixing bowl, dissolve the sea salt in the 4 cups of warm water. Set aside until cool.

Add garlic and dill to saltwater brine.

Add your carrots or cucumbers to the jar. Pickling cucumbers will stay crisper longer but you can use table cucumbers.

Pour the brine over the vegetables in the jars, leaving ½-1 inch of space at the top.

For each jar, fold a small cabbage leaf so that it fits snugly into the jar and press it into the brine so that it is completely submerged and covers the vegetables or put a canning weight on top of the vegetables.

I put coffee filters over the top of the lids and secure with either a rubber band around the mouth of the jar or tie it with a string.
Place the jars in a location out of direct sunlight.

Ferment the vegetables for 1-4 days, tasting the vegetables daily to see if you think they are tangy enough. There should be bubbles on the surface of the saltwater.

You can let them ferment for as long as you want until they taste the way you like. 2-3 days is typical. The length of time it will take to ferment will change depending on how warm it is in your house or the time of year.

Once your veggies taste like you want them to, take off the coffee filter and put on a regular lid.

Store them in the refrigerator. They will last for 2-3 months in the fridge but you will probably eat them too fast for them to be there for long.

If they ever look "off", have mold on them or smell bad then discard that batch and start a new one.

You can also use the brine in place of some of your vinegar in homemade salad dressings or dips or even put a tsp in a strong flavored juice or mix into fruit puree to get the beneficial bacteria. This is a good way to get more good bacteria into children or picky adults!

Gut Healing

Bone Broth

Bone broth is very healing for your gut. It is rich in collagen and minerals. Bone broth will help heal leaky gut and has an entire host of health benefits for your body.

If you are very constipated you can do a bone broth fast, only drinking bone broth, until your constipation abates.

I use bone broth in many different recipes. I use it instead of water when I make rice, in homemade soups and I even put a couple of cups of bone broth in tomato sauce when I make spaghetti.

Ingredients:

Organic chicken or beef bones

I use the carcass of a chicken but any scrap bones can be used. Chicken feet and necks are great for added collagen.

Scrap vegetables such as carrots, celery, onion, garlic.

I keep a ziplock bag in the freezer and add veggie scraps throughout the week. When I make bone broth, I pull out the bag and dump the scraps in with the bones.

1 TBS organic Apple Cider Vinegar with the Mother.

I also add herbs such as nettles, thyme, parsley, and rosemary but this is optional.

Put the bones and veggies in a large stockpot or crockpot and cover with water.

Add ACV. The vinegar will help get vitamins and minerals out of the bones.

Bring to a boil and skim off any sludge that forms on the surface.

Lower the heat to medium-low and simmer for 4-24 hours. Beef bones generally take longer to cook than chicken bones.

Strain out the bones, herbs, and veggies and put in glass jars.

Store in the refrigerator.

Use throughout the week in your recipes or drink the broth instead of coffee or tea.

Tomato Soup

Tomato soup can be made quickly and is a favorite in my family. I always have jars of bone broth in my refrigerator ready to make this soup.

Ingredients:

4 cups bone broth

4 cups chopped tomatoes, either fresh or canned.

1 TBS chopped basil

1 tsp Celtic Sea Salt

½ tsp pepper

Add all ingredients into a pot and cook on medium heat for 25 minutes stirring frequently.

Using a stick blender, blend the soup until smooth. If you do not have a stick blender, blend the tomatoes prior to adding to the pot. It is difficult to blend the hot soup in a blender as it will expand and can burn you when you take off the lid.

Lemon Chicken Soup

Lemon Chicken soup is another wonderful soup that is tasty and healing for your gut.

You get the benefit of the bone broth to heal your gut, fiber, and vitamins from spinach, and lemons, sulfur from onion and minerals from Celtic Sea Salt.

> 4 cups cooked shredded chicken.

This is about the amount of chicken you can get from one rotisserie chicken if you would like to use that instead of cooking your own chicken. Using a rotisserie chicken makes this a quick weeknight meal.

> 6 cups bone broth
>
> 2 cups chopped spinach
>
> Zest from 2 lemons
>
> 2 TBS fresh lemon juice
>
> 1 cup chopped onion
>
> 1/2 cup olive oil
>
> Celtic Sea Salt to taste

Add 2 cups of stock, chopped onion, 1 cup chopped spinach, and olive oil to blender. Blend until smooth.

Add blended stock mixture and the remaining 4 cups of broth, spinach, shredded chicken, zest of two lemons, 2 TBS of fresh lemon juice and salt to taste to the pot.

Cook on medium-low for 1 hour.

Coconut Oil Poop Candy

Coconut Oil Poop Candy

Coconut Oil Poop Candy is wonderful for constipation relief.

I love Coconut Oil. I go through gallons of it a year. I use it topically in homemade creams, lotions, and makeup removers and for rashes, burns or other skin irritation. I also use it for cooking and baking.

I especially love it for gluten-free baking because it makes whatever you are making soft with a beautiful texture. Gluten-free products can get dry very quickly and I have found that using coconut oil in baking keeps the baked goods softer longer as well.

It handles high heat so is excellent for frying food.

Cold-pressed Virgin Coconut oil is incredibly good for you. It is antimicrobial and anti-fungal so it can help when you are battling fungal or bacterial issues.

Coconut Oil is Very Effective for Constipation Relief.

Coconut oil is rich in Medium Chain Fatty Acids. MCFA's boost your metabolism which makes the stool pass through your intestines faster, the oil coats and lubricates harder old stool making it easier to pass. Coconut oil also softens newly formed stool making it easier to pass.

If you are struggling with long-term constipation issues or just get backed up occasionally, I highly recommend adding coconut oil to your diet.

There are many ways to enjoy coconut oil. Instead of using other oils in your cooking or baking, you can use coconut oil, you can use it instead of butter on toast or veggies, you can add it to your hot beverages like coffee or tea. Some people just eat it directly off the spoon. It has a mild, almost sweet flavor.

It can be tricky to get enough coconut oil into children who are struggling with constipation. Especially children with sensory issues or autism or ones who just don't like the taste of coconut oil.

One of the easiest ways I have found to get children to eat enough coconut oil to relieve constipation is with my famous Coconut Oil Poop Candy.

Original Chocolate Coconut Oil "Poop Candy"

Use equal parts of chocolate chips to coconut oil. 1 cup to 1 cup or 1/2 cup to 1/2 cup. I use chocolate chips are gluten-free and dairy-free. Gluten and dairy are common causes of constipation.

If you are going to make a lot of these, a double boiler is really handy. If you don't have one, you can make a makeshift double boiler with a Pyrex bowl over a pan. Add a couple of inches of water to the pan, put the bowl over the pan.

Heat on low heat while stirring the chocolate/coconut oil mixture until it melts. Once it is smooth and lump-free, pour it into a silicone candy mold, ice cube tray or cupcake papers.

Carefully put the filled mold in the refrigerator or freezer until the chocolates are firm.

The silicone molds can bend so it often helps to put the mold on a plate or cookie sheet before you add the chocolate so you can carry it to the fridge without spilling it.

It usually takes less 30 minutes for the candies to harden depending on the size of the mold. Then pop the chocolates out and serve.

The chocolates that are leftover need to be stored in the fridge or freezer. They melt quickly and can be messy.

My son isn't much of a sweet eater but he loves these.

One of my readers shared "I made these a week ago. My son is 8. I did 2 in the morning and 2 in the afternoon and it took about 3 full days for results. But since then we have had a BM every day…..finally! Yay!"

Chocolate Coconut Oil Poop Candy

1 cup organic coconut oil

1 cup organic dairy-free chocolate chips

Melt in a double boiler or in a heat-safe bowl over a pan of boiling water.

Stir until melted and smooth.

Pour into molds

Place in the refrigerator or freezer until solid.

Store in an airtight container in the refrigerator or freezer.

Eat 2-5 every 2 hours until you have a bowel movement. The number of candies it will take to produce a bowel movement depends on the size of the molds you use and how constipated you are.

Peanut Butter Cup Poop Candy

Peanut Butter Cup "Poop Candy"

- 3/4 Cup Chocolate Chips
- 1/4 Cup Peanut Butter
- 1 Cup Coconut Oil, divided
- Celtic Sea Salt to taste

In your bowl over a pot of water or double boiler, mix 3/4 cup chocolate chips with 3/4 cup coconut oil and melt over medium heat until smooth.

Place the mold on a plate to make it easier to transfer the candy to the freezer.

Optional: add a sprinkle of Course Ground Celtic Sea Salt to the mold.

Pour half of your chocolate mixture into your silicone mold.

Put the mold into the freezer for 10-15 minutes until the chocolate is firm.

In a second bowl or in your cleaned double boiler, mix together 1/4 cup peanut butter and 1/4 cup coconut oil and melt over medium heat until smooth.

Pour peanut butter mixture on top of the chocolate mixture and put in the freezer until firm, 10-15 minutes.

Remove from the freezer and reheat the second half of the chocolate mixture until smooth. Pour the remaining chocolate mixture over the peanut butter layer and return the freezer until firm.

Pop the chocolates out and serve.

The chocolates that are leftover need to be stored in the fridge or freezer. They melt quickly and can be messy.

Some people use a microwave to melt the chocolate and peanut butter mixtures but I am concerned that it would damage some of the healing properties of the coconut oil so I always use the double boiler method.

Peppermint Poop Candy

Put 1 cup of peppermint candies in a zip lock bag and crush the candies. You can use a mallet or a rolling pin.

You can make this in silicone molds, muffin papers or as bark by pouring it onto parchment paper on a cookie sheet.

Sprinkle some crushed candy in the mold.

In a double boiler, melt 1 cup chocolate chips and 1 cup of coconut oil.

Stir the chocolate coconut oil mixture until it melts. Once it is smooth and lump-free, pour it into a silicone candy mold.

Sprinkle the rest of the crushed candy onto the chocolate mixture.

Carefully put the filled mold in the refrigerator or freezer until the chocolates are firm.

It usually takes less 30 minutes for them to harden depending on the size of the mold. Then pop the chocolates out and serve.

The leftover chocolate needs to be stored in the fridge or freezer. They melt quickly and can be messy.

Coconut Free Poop Candy

My Coconut Poop Candy is tasty and effective but what if you can't have coconut or you don't like the taste of coconut?

After doing some recipe testing I discovered that palm oil works as a wonderful substitute for coconut oil.

Ingredients:

1 cup organic Palm Oil

1 cup dairy-free chocolate chips

Melt in a double boiler or in a heat-safe bowl over a pan of boiling water.

Stir until melted and smooth. Pour into molds

Place in the refrigerator or freezer until solid.

Store in an airtight container in the refrigerator or freezer. These seem to be less "melty" than the coconut oil poop candies but held up better in the fridge than left out on the counter.

Eat 2-5 every 2 hours until you have a bowel movement. The number of candies it will take to produce a bowel movement depends on the size of the molds you use and how constipated you are.

Nut or Seed Butter Poop Candy

1 cup peanut butter or other nut or seed butter

1 cup of coconut oil

Melt in a double boiler or in a heat-safe bowl over a pan of boiling water.

Stir until melted and smooth. Pour into molds

Place in the refrigerator or freezer until solid.

Store in an airtight container in the refrigerator or freezer.

Eat 2-5 every 2 hours until you have a bowel movement. The number of candies it will take to produce a bowel movement depends on the size of the molds you use and how constipated you are.

Berry Poop Candy

Ingredients:

1 cup refined coconut oil

1/2 cup of frozen berries, such as raspberries, blueberries, pomegranates, cherries, or strawberries.

1 teaspoon vanilla extract

1 TBS honey

Instructions:

Heat coconut oil in a pot until melted.

While the oil is melting, briefly process the frozen fruit in a food processor or blender so it's chopped up into small pieces.

Add the vanilla extract and honey to your food processor or blender.

Pour the melted coconut oil into your food processor or blender and process to mix with the fruit and other ingredients.

The mixture should now be a thick blended consistency.

Scoop mixture into a silicone mold or ice cube tray.

Put molds into the freezer for 30 minutes until firm.

Lemon Poop Candy

Ingredients:

1 cup of coconut oil

2 1/2 teaspoons lemon zest, approximately one lemon's worth

1/4 cup lemon juice

2 tablespoons honey

Instructions:

Gently melt ½ cup coconut oil in a pan on the stove.

Add zest and lemon juice to your food processor or blender.

Add melted and unmelted coconut oil to your food processor or blender.

Add honey.

Process until all ingredients until smooth.

Scoop finished mixture into molds.

Put molds into the freezer to firm up the Lemon Poop Candy for 15-30 minutes.

Topical Constipation Remedies

Magnesium

Magnesium is one of the quickest and most effective ways to help your child or an adult with their constipation. It is estimated that 50-80% of people are magnesium deficient. This number is probably even higher if you are dealing with constipation.

Even if you aren't dealing with a deficiency, most people aren't in the optimal range for magnesium.

You can take magnesium by mouth, like in my Electrolyte Drink recipe, but you can also absorb magnesium through your skin. Epsom salt baths are a great way to do this.

Another really helpful way to use magnesium externally is by using magnesium for a tummy massage. You can do this on yourself but it is much easier to have someone do it for you if that is an option.

Generally, using magnesium topically doesn't have the same laxative effect that taking magnesium by mouth does. But many families have reported a lot of success using magnesium and massage to get a bowel movement.

When your magnesium stores are full, it takes very little magnesium to get a laxative effect. Anything you can do to increase magnesium stores will benefit anyone struggling with constipation.

Magnesium and tummy massage is a very effective weapon in your arsenal against constipation.

Magnesium Oil

Magnesium Oil used externally will help increase your magnesium stores so it will take less magnesium citrate or other types of magnesium to get a bowel movement.

Magnesium Oil:

Measure out 1/2 cup of Magnesium Chloride flakes and 3 Tablespoons of filtered water and put in a pan.

Heat on medium-low heat until the flakes dissolve.

Store in a glass spray bottle.

This is magnesium oil, super easy! It isn't actually an oil even though it is commonly called an oil but it has an oily texture.

Magnesium oil can be very drying and can sting when you use it on your skin. It stings less when used on the soles of the feet or on places on the body with more fat if you want to use it like this. It can also leave a white residue and can dry and irritate the skin. If you use the oil you can bathe or wipe off the reside 30 minutes after applying.

Magnesium Cream

Magnesium Cream works like Magnesium Oil but doesn't sting and doesn't dry the skin the way magnesium oil does. It is a few more steps but my family really loves using Magnesium Cream.

Rubbing Magnesium Cream on the soles of your feet or your child's feet before bed can help with sleep as well as build up magnesium stores in your body. You can also use this magnesium cream to do a tummy massage to help stimulate the intestines to push out a bowel movement.

To make the Magnesium Cream:

Melt 1/4 Cup of Organic Coconut Oil on your stove over low heat in a double boiler or in a heat-safe bowl over a pan of boiling water.

Add 1/4 Cup of Organic Shea Butter.

Put the mixture in the refrigerator until it is solid. I put it in my mixing bowl and then put it in the fridge.

After it is solid, which takes just a few minutes, take it out of the refrigerator and add 1/4 cup of the Magnesium Oil you made, or some you have purchased, to your mixing bowl.

Use your whisk attachment if you have one. It will whip the cream and make it fluffy and silky.

Slowly increase the speed of your mixer until your cream is forming peaks like whipped cream, then turn your mixer off. This should take 2-5 minutes depending on your mixer and on the temperature of your house and of the ingredients.

Transfer your cream to a glass jar.

Storing it in your fridge will keep the cream with a whipped texture and keep it fresh for months.

Coconut oil becomes a liquid at room temperature so if you leave it in your bedroom or bathroom this cream will deflate and become more solid. You can still use it but it isn't as nice of a texture.

1 teaspoon of this magnesium cream = 250 mg of Magnesium.

Magnesium Cream Massage for Constipation Relief

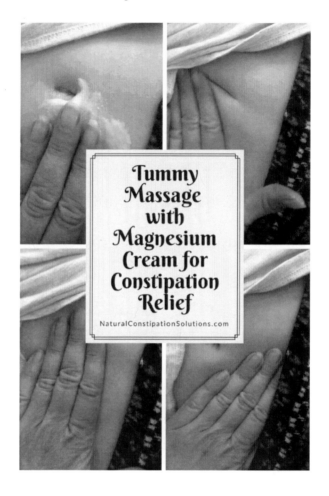

Once you have your cream done, you can massage it into your stomach or your child's tummy.

There are a lot of videos on YouTube that show you how to do a belly massage for constipation but the main idea is to put 1-2 tsp of cream on your or your child's tummy. Press with a flat hand and move gently but firmly clockwise in a circular motion, expanding out from your bellybutton for 5-20 minutes.

Don't press so hard that it is uncomfortable, but press with a firm touch. This will help move the gas and stool in your gut.

If you are doing this with your child, you can also take your child's legs and bring their knees up to their chest and press gently.

At the first sign of them having to go, get them on the potty and have them try. This will often move the gas and stool around and help it to be released.

If doing the massage to yourself, raise your knees and hug them into your chest.

You can do the tummy massage a couple of times a day and you can use the magnesium cream daily to work on building up the stores of this vital mineral.

Castor Oil Packs for Constipation Relief

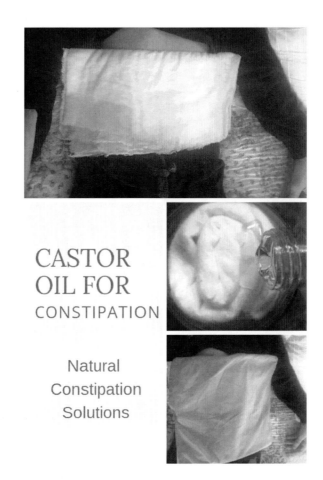

Castor oil has been used medically for thousands of years. There is evidence of it being used by Ancient Egyptians. Generations of mothers have used Castor oil for constipation relief for their families. When something has been used for thousands of years, it generally shows that it is safe and effective.

Castor oil works as a stimulant laxative when taken internally. Castor oil is 90% ricinoleic acid. The ricinoleic acid causes smooth muscle contractions in your intestines, pushing the stool through your intestines and helping you to have a bowel movement.

When you take castor oil by mouth, it is a very effective laxative. It has a very strong taste and is a thick texture that isn't pleasant so it isn't the most pleasant way to use Castor oil.

Side effects of using Castor oil internally can include cramping and digestive upset. Do not use if pregnant or breastfeeding. If pregnant it can cause contractions and stimulate labor.

When you take Castor oil internally it works fairly quickly, usually within 2-6 hours so do not give too closely to bedtime as it will interrupt sleep with needing to use the bathroom multiple times.

It causes very strong contractions and the urge to go. It can be difficult to make it to the restroom when you take it internally.

Instead of using Castor oil by mouth, you can use it in a Castor oil pack. A Castor oil pack is made with cotton flannel fabric that has been saturated with Castor oil and is placed over your stomach with a heating pad placed on top.

Doing a Castor oil pack is messy so you will want an old t-shirt or scrap cloth between the flannel and your heating pad.

Take your flannel and fold it and then roll it so it fits in a glass jar such as a quart-sized Ball jar.

Add 1/4 cup of Castor oil to the flannel and let sit for 20 minutes. Add 1-2 TBS every 20 minutes until your flannel is saturated but not dripping. This can take hours or even a day to reach saturation so you might want to do this the day before needing it.

Lie down on an old towel if you are concerned that the flannel might leak Castor oil on your bed or couch.

Unfold the flannel and place it on the lower abdomen over the intestines.

Place an old towel, an old t-shirt that you don't care about or even some plastic wrap over the flannel and then put the hot water bottle or heating pad over the flannel. If using a hot water bottle it may need to be reheated several times.

Leave on the Castor oil pack for 30 minutes to two hours.

You can reuse your flannel many times, often up to 30 or 35 times before needing to replace the flannel with a new cloth.

After each use, just add a TBS or two of Castor oil to the folded up flannel in the jar and let it soak in until you use it the next time.

Store in the refrigerator until next use.

Use daily for constipation relief. Using a Castor oil pack won't work as quickly as taking castor oil internally so you will need some patience to use it as a pack for constipation, but it is very effective for some people.

If you enjoyed these recipes, please leave a review on Amazon.

If you need more support, please visit my website:
NaturalConstipationSolutions.com

Made in United States
North Haven, CT
27 December 2022